ETERNAL ECHOES

The Sacred
sounds through the Mystic

Poems by

SADHGURU JAGGI VASUDEV

ETERNAL ECHOES

ISBN No : 81-87910-02-X

Published by: **Isha Foundation**
15, Govindasamy Naidu Layout
Singanallur, Coimbatore – 641 005 INDIA

e-mail: yogacentre@ishafoundation.org
website: www.ishafoundation.org

Design by : **Isha Foundation**

First Edition: May 2002

Gratitude to the Master

This restless species that we are
Wonders what past perils bound us

And what present miracle
Delivered us to your feet

You have loosened the shackles
And we are grateful for

The love that lessens
The madness of our quest

With loving gratitude of millions of devotees, disciples and seekers of Truth
whose hearts have been touched by our beloved Sadhguru Jaggi Vasudev

Contents

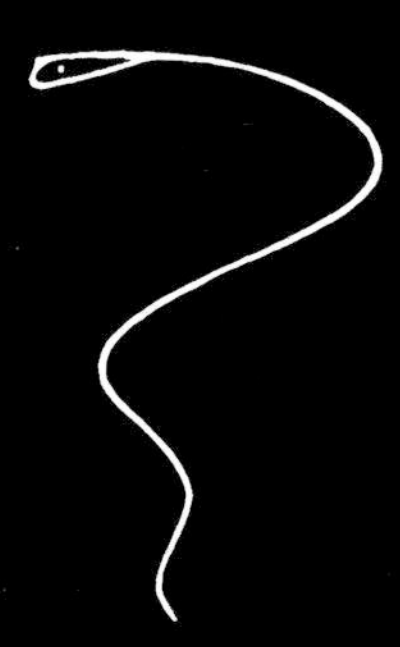

Preface

The entire phenomenon of life and existence is largely beyond the definition of the rational and logical. The enigmatic poetry of yogi, master and mystic Sadhguru has the potential to guide us on our evolutionary progression towards the ultimate.

In the richness of expression of his verse are lyrical insights into a timeless, eternal reality. **Eternal Echoes'** eloquent sounds of life both sacred and profane create space to allow the mind to float. They are both ethereal in their message and earthy in their sensuality.

A poem becomes poetry only when it says something that has not been said, when something about it transcends the parts. If divided and analyzed, then only parts remain; the transcendental song that was intended is lost.

Likewise yoga is the science of transcending parts so that we may become whole. It is the harmony of art and science - totally rational yet moving us deeply into the mystery of the irrational.

Introduction

Even as a small child, verse came naturally to the illumined being known as Sadhguru Jaggi Vasudev, whose presence flows from the very source of creation. Recognized as a great yogi, mystic and master, Sadhguru reveals his vital identification with the Divine and communicates love for humanity through his compelling and provocative poetry.

Mystics like Sadhguru have access to realms of realization that are usually cloaked from most. We frequently find that only verse is suitable for giving expression to what is beyond the senses. Through the ineffable sharing of this poetry we get a glimpse into his experience of enlightenment.

In **Eternal Echoes**, the Master's sacred poetry uses language as revelation, and is often a penetrating cluster of meaning, brevity and intensity. Not just beautiful prose and random musings, his poetry is an outpouring of subtle truths with relevancy that pierces our inner core.

When reading Sadhguru's poetry, we must activate the intelligence of the heart. For to lose ourselves in the outward sense of his words, the inner truth would be missed. Those willing to savor his language of spirit will gain a glimpse of the infinite formless Divine - Isha.

As evident in his enlivening outward character, the Master's poetry dances. The flow, rhythm and impact of this collection of Sadhguru's poetic sounds are divided into three segments: his offerings to seekers of truth in **Beyond Love** ; his Divine dispensation in the form of Yoga in **The Divine Secret**; and his intoxicating intimacy with the inner and outer realms of life in **Glimpse of the Master.**

Echoed in the primitive throb of the dance is his true intention – to challenge and guide us to the eternal possibility within us all.

Beyond Love

Isha, the formless Divine, is the name reflecting the essence of the work of Sadhguru. In **Beyond Love**, all devotees, disciples and seekers of Truth are addressed by the Master as Ishas – seeds of divine potentiality.

From his infancy, Sadhguru always had an imprint of mountains in his eyes. Though he wandered much of India in search of sacred land to host his immortal work, it was only the Velliangiri Mountains of South India that matched his inner vision. The burning desire to fulfill his Guru's will led the Self before him to shed his body on Velliangiri's sacred seventh hill with the revelation, "This One will be back." In his present form, Sadhguru continues the legacy of three enlightened lifetimes now manifest at these foothills. Here he established the Isha Yoga Center as sacred space for spiritual unfoldment, open to individuals seeking to evolve themselves to their ultimate nature.

A Guru is not a teacher who can pass on something to people; he is someone who includes them as part of himself. That is the only way he can make them whole. As expressed vividly in "**Tread Gently**," the Master is like a womb for us to be born again.

Sadhguru challenges us to leap beyond our abasements in "**Unmaking**," yet he shows us that his heart is large enough to carry the whole of existence in his eternal promise, "**Across**" - a poem penned at a time when his energy body was in a state of damage due to the consecration process of the Linga.

Sadhguru invites us to be aware of limiting forms in "**Beyond Love**," and then leaves us with an image of the unlimited oneness of reality. The Master moves with spirited delight in his inner knowing in "**Firefly**" and enchants us with simplicity in the whimsical "**Of Snowflakes and Me**." Yet always Sadhguru remains a synthesis of life, an all-encompassing sage revealing the intimate relationship and energy bond between Guru and disciple so mystically expressed in "**Bliss**" and "**Become Me**."

Mystical poetry often functions as an element to disturb our complacency. "**Pain**" speaks of resistance and forces us to reflect on its impact on the spiritual preceptor. Sadhguru's poetry clearly shows what a tremendous possibility his Being offers all yearning to evolve to freedom, total being and pure consciousness. For all who seek refuge from the superficial life, Sadhguru is an open door. His heart is our passage to the eternal that exists within.

Tread Gently

Tread gently O' Ishas!
I've let you seep into
The minute crevices of my body
Where life entrenched itself

Encompassing you all into this
Pulsating mass of flesh
I've become eternally pregnant

This rapture, this pain, this fullness
I am unable to bear, but love and longing
Will never let you part

This flesh, blood, breath and being
Are soaked with you

Your every thought, word and deed
Penetrates the life preserving crevices of the body

Tread in love, compassion and awareness
For all that you tread is only me

Senses and senses meet to leave one
Senseless of all that is true
The door that blocks
Is also the door that liberates
Which side of the door you are
Is all there is
Shambho, my doughtiness and your grace
Got me to your side of the door
If you are too choosy
As to who should cross this door
A mistake with me you made
This new sense has left me so senseless
That I will keep this door open
For every vermin that can crawl and cross
Pardon me my treacherous arrogance
As I am only you

Beyond Love

This universe is but a minuscule
In the vastness of my inner spaces

My love for you is but a ploy
To retain this little toy (body)

I know neither love nor longing
As all that is, is me

You an unlimited possibility
Have settled to be a limited diversity

Your exclusiveness, you enshrined
But my inclusiveness cannot be chained

When it is just me, me and me alone
Why this you and me?

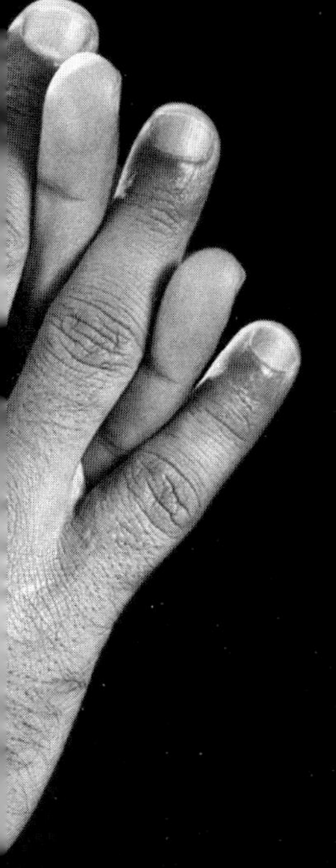

Become Me

I was borne in my Mother's womb
but she did not create me

I eat the salt of this earth
but I do not belong to her

It is through this body that I walk
but I am not it

It is my mind through which I work
but it could not contain me

In the limitations of time and space I live
but it has not denied me unboundedness

I was born like you, I eat like you,
sleep like you and I will die like you
but the limited has not limited me
Life's bondages have not bound me
As the dance of life progresses
this space, this unboundedness has become
unbearably sweet

Become love and reach out
Become me

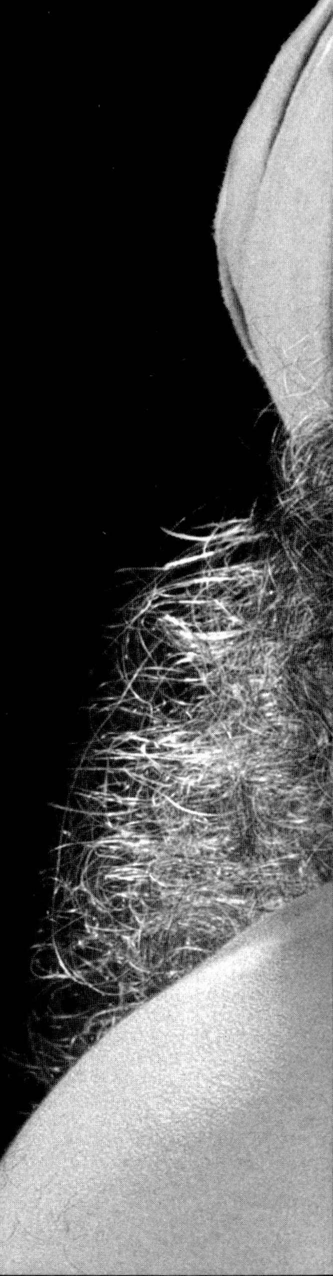

Across

This boat of many holes
The reckless sailor that I am
Have set upon oceans vast
Plugging the holes with people's lives
"I've hoisted the flag of hope.
Can't let it sink, you see."
The sail is torn, the mast broken
The rudder has gone asunder
This boat powered only by my longing to share
Navigated by the Grace of my deepest hidden love
This rickety boat held together only by your heart strings
And still I say, "I'll see you across."

Unmaking

Those who feed upon the written word
Claim to know the limits of the boundless beyond

In the realm of the beyond
Clueless is the scholarly dud

The gloriousness of the written word
Is but the excreta of the deluded mind

If in you a raging longing I have made
Don't you quench it with the delusions of the mind

Allow yourself to be unmade
Into the vastness of the beyond you will be made

Bliss

In faraway lands am I
But as near to you as ever
I've infused my life energies in you
And you are no more yourself but me
You are among the privileged few
Who seek the Creator

My blissfulness is my only blessing
You should know the bliss that is me

Isha

The mountain peaks that haunted me from infancy
At their feet now I set you down
Many a seeker's deep longing
Impelled me to set a part of me
At the foothills of these sacred mountains
These mountains where seers and sages walked
The most glorious one, my light and liberation
Chose these magnificent peaks to dissolve

Now at their feet a sturdy band
Of seekers are pursuing the timeless, immortal path
Their seeking and longing
Their struggle and joy
Their pain and love
I bear in my heart
These wondrous creatures, these Ishas
Sure shall bring light to the world

Firefly

In the dark moonless night
The firefly emboldens itself to flight

The brooding darkness mocks
The spirited flight of fly delight

The limitless darkness could
Swallow this minuscule attempt of light

The skeptics' cantankerous laughter
Swept the inner spaces within me
To ask: Can a firefly light the world?

Yes firefly am I
If life's summers have warmed you
Your inner spaces have charmed you
I could set you afire and the world too

Pai

My pain is not of the wounded
Nor is this the pain of the lost
Nor of defeat and failure
This the pain of the mother
When the one in her womb turned against her
She would be willing to go
Just to let him be
If she lets go she will kill
If she reaches out she will kill
This the pain of knowing
In your love you will destroy
In your withdrawal you will destroy
That which is but your part
Till the part is willing to be the whole
The pain will take its toll
This true of creation and me

Of Snowflakes and Me

The snowflakes white and light
They say are falling heavy tonight

As I walk with an upturned face
To receive their fragile grace

Me wonder if the heaven is falling apart
Or just in a flaky freakout

Must be heavens falling out
To spring back at spring

Me a snowflake too
As fragile and grace

If you have an upturned face
Me fall to spring back in heaven's grace

The Divine Secret

Yoga – The Divine Secret – this sacred science of unraveling the Divine in every being. Sadhguru adheres to no particular religion or belief system, but has chosen yoga as the vehicle to self-realization. In a deeper dimension yoga is the very basis and process of his life epic spanning three lifetimes.

Encompassing dimensions before and beyond this life, "**Shiva**" confirms that Sadhguru's every action was guided and guarded by the Illustrious One, Shambho – both the Divine initiator and destroyer. In the yogic tradition, Shiva is considered the Adi (first) Guru. Sadhguru does not use Shiva in the context of a god or deity, but as a device to relate to that which is beyond duality. In sacred mythology, Shiva has been described as the most beautiful and the most terrible. If we can accept Shiva, we accept the totality of life.

The Master's journey through three lifetimes began with a yogi's search for the Ultimate and culminated in the highest physical manifestation of Divinity – a fusion of the infinite and finite revealed in "**Linga**." Dhyanalinga is the distilled essence of yogic science, but as evident in the poem by the same name, definitions defy the magnificence of this phenomenon that springs from the very source of existence. In the metaphysical sense, Dhyanalinga is the manifestation of a Guru, an eternal energy center of tremendous proportions and a space where transformation from limited to resplendent unbounded can happen in an instant.

The intense sadhana necessary to bring Dhyanalinga to fruition took its toll on the Master's body. Although disciples were prepared for him to leave this physical existence at the consecration of Dhyanalinga, their love and longing was the catalyst for the Master to stay, and guiding them to liberation remains the primary impetus for Sadhguru to retain his body for some more time, as poignantly expressed in "**Tenderness**."

The poems "**Shiva**" and "**Imbecile**" alert us to the fierce reverence and devotion the Master shows for his Guru's will. His commitment beyond life and death is described as an obsession in "**Dhyanalinga**," yet finds a worthy expression in "**The Glorious One**."

Mystics often say definitions are futile because what is beyond our experience cannot be understood. But even an effort that is futile can share a glimpse of the Divine Secret and lead us to the threshold of Truth. Sadhguru's description of his Divinity in "**Here and Here**" is one such opening to help us know the unknowable.

o

Yoga

Your face is hard
They think you are a loveless wench
To me you are like a lover's song
Gentle as the spring breeze.
Like a mango tree in full bloom
Every leaf hides a delicious fruit.
Such bare and scarce ways did your progenitor describe you...
Folks would never know the luscious lass that you are
Clothed in rough and common raiment
Who could dream of the uncommon possibility that you are?
I spied and pursued you with a stout heart
Waiting and wooing for life times three
Trailing you through terrain unknown
Of untold pain and sweetness too
The very journey has left me so complete
The creation and creator are within me
Can no more see the world without you.

Shiva

You drew two lines for everyone
Betwixt which to live their lives

But just one for me

To see that I don't cross YOU
I am willing to cross the whole creation

You made me in your own mould
Infused me with your fire

My longing and your will
To warm this world with your fire

But the warmth of your fires
Could burn the lifeless infidels

That they will name me the evil
And in turn YOU

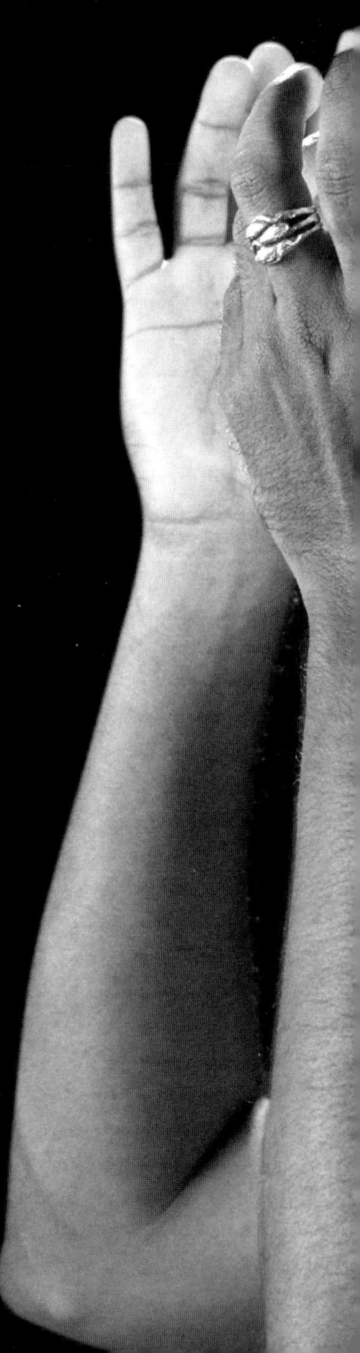

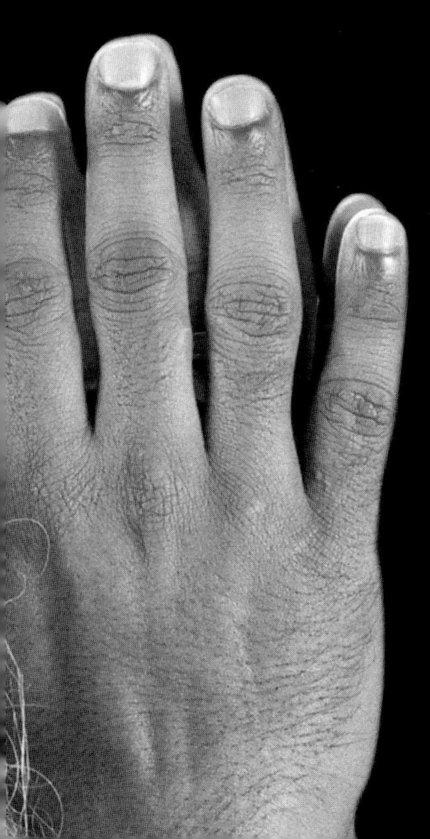

Dhyanalinga

You are my Guru's will
My only obsession
In my dreams and my wakefulness
My only longing was to fulfill you

Willing to do anything
That men should and should not
Willing to offer myself and
Another hundred lives if need be

Here now that you have happened
O' Glorious One
May your Glory and Grace
Stir the sleeping hordes
Into wakefulness and light

Now that you have happened
And the gift of life still with me
What shall I do with myself

Have lived the peaks for too long
Time to graze the valleys of life

Tenderness

The irony of life
That I should now
Be doing everything to bind myself
To demarcate boundaries
That no one should cross.
Doing my best to be self-centered.

All these antics just to keep
This crumbling cage intact.
'With the work done
Why linger on?
Depart gracefully,' says my mind.

But what to do with lovers
Who have lost themselves in the
Process of loving.
Too many lovers, the very remembrance
Bring tears of too much tenderness
So I'll act brash and go on.

Limitless

The limitless energy
Dances in many limited ways

The limited so complete
That it thinks it is its own

The limited and the limitless
Where is the line, unless you draw one

The illusion of the limited
The source of longing and pain

A taste of the unlimited leaves you
Drenched in Bliss Divine

Makes the pleasure and pain of life
Sweeter by the million

Absence

If you are enamoured with my presence
O' you should taste my absence

If my presence has made some sense
In my absence you would know the true essence

In my presence if you did find some romance
My absence would bring you to utter obeisance

In my presence if you have been swept by my grace
My absence will take you beyond grace and disgrace

If my presence has been an intoxicating wine
My absence will drown you in Divine

The Glorious One

In your limitless abode you sit
Like you are the very center of the Universe
All the loving hands that toiled to
Make dome divine your domain
Are blessed with blissful owners

As I enter this domain divine for the thousandth time
My spine tingles with sensations
That a young lass wouldn't have dreamt of

Sensations that will melt
Stony hearts to pulp
Blaze dim beings into beings of light
Transform weaklings into powerhouses
The wretched into virtuous
The joyless into blissful
Raise cowards into the realm of the fearless
For the one who has known these
Divine sensations of Dhyanalinga

The glories of life will play at his feet

Linga

You are the firstborn
The first expression of the cosmic emptiness

The wise ones espied you
To be the source of all this lively mischief

You are the source of all pain and pleasure
You are the lowest and the highest

Ah, the games that you play
The multitude of forms for which you are the source
Are neither this nor that

I wormed through creation
To discover you and me

O' Ishana the most glorious form
Blessed is Isha to be your abode

My awareness knows yesterdays and tomorrows
My love's domain is only today
Knowing the beginning and the end
Still have to play the game in the middle

The joy of love was coupled with life taking venom
The wondrous grace of the guru
With heart breaking sadhana

The fire of enlightenment with ridicule and failure
The blissfulness of the being, the rapture of
Fulfillment enjoined with the pain of the body

Is this a joke?
This is Shiva's will?
Is he compassion or cruel?

O' Shambho! Let me tell one and all
I do not want it any other way
I do not want it any other way!

Imbecile

O'Shambho
You made me yours
Setting a purpose and pitch
The guileless me fell for your charm
And took on much that is beyond me
When I saw that you were a little too much
I did apply you to the world
And the world was willing too
There is nothing here that is me or mine
Took everyone as mine as they were yours
This imbecile me has no will of my own
Let me not do that which would disgrace you
You chose me, you directed me, you set me forth
You chose to make this imbecile
Your lowly part

I have no will of my own
Make me your lowly part

Here and Here

These people want to know who I am
These children of God
Drunk upon the fruit of ignorance
Want to know where I come from

These pearly dewdrops
That hang precariously from the
Blades of grass. I'm in them.

The lovely fresh orange blossom
Of the spring. I'm in them.

The silent songs of these timeless
rocks. I'm in that.

The ageold scent of the
Cedars. I'm in that.

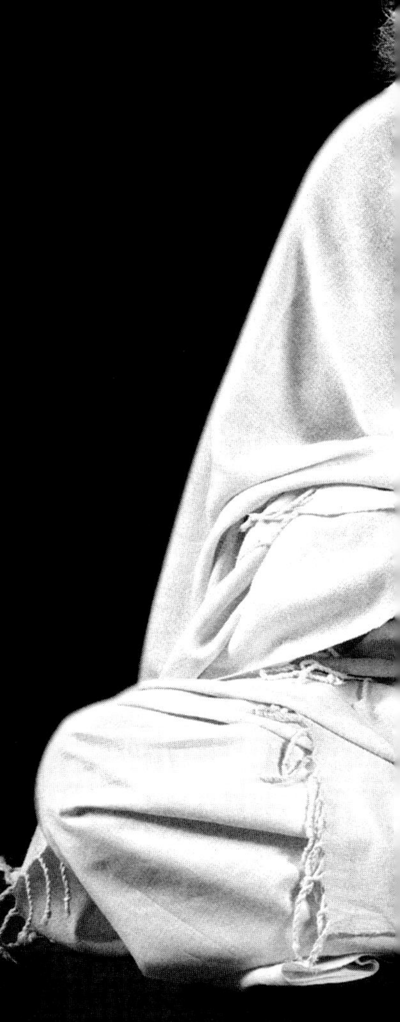

The sweetness that the mother's breast
Bares for the child. I'm in that.

The coyotes howling away their ancient
Sorrows. I'm in that.

Where is there for me to come from
Where is there to go

All has become stillness
As everything that's moving
And unmoving is me.

Glimpse of the Master

The very urge to seek comes after we have tasted something beyond the barrier of reason – even a glimpse. Within the poems in **Glimpse of the Master**, Sadhguru provides the impetus to jump into the impossible by sharing some enigmatic encounters with his Self.

Although he speaks of worldly homelessness in "**Boundless**," Sadhguru is at home wherever he is. Whether in his personal gardens at the foothills of his beloved Velliangiri Mountains, in the woods of Tennessee or traversing the globe, he relates to life beyond the limited expression of physical reality.

Ever since the spiritual dimension became live in him, the Master was drawn to the Himalayas, not for spiritual pursuits, but as a return to his mystical home. Even modern attire could not cloak his divinity from countless Himalayan mountain yogis, who recognized him and sought initiation. "**Himalaya**" expresses the Master's timeless connection with this enlightened land and inhabitants, the Dwijas, who have attained self-realization among its peaks.

The Master's compassion transcends space and time and is inclusive of all dimensions of life, as evident in his deep connection with nature in "**One and the Same**," his encounter with Native American disembodied beings in rural Tennessee in "**America**" and his interaction with antiquity in the mountains of Lebanon in "**Life**."

A living teacher of Truth is liquid; he can change into anything needed to do his work. In "**The Dark One**" the Master reveals the depth of his being beyond any boundary. Yet to effectively reach out to those willing, he admits in "**me and Me**", that this One is often covered by a façade carefully crafted to lead us beyond our limitations.

In all his roles, the Master manifests what is required at the moment with the uncanny ability to purely and perfectly respond to each situation and person. "**Shameless**" is a graphic appeal for us to shed our hypocrisy and ignorance so that he can ignite the ultimate possibility within.

Sadhguru's love is not a human emotion but a joyous attempt to awaken in us the realization that we are indeed one with existence. Giving himself totally, responding freely and purely, his impact draws like a magnet those wanting to dissolve into the beauty and love of interaction.

me and Me

The impish me
And the absolute ME

Many think a contradiction
But a perfect complement

My love, my joy, my laughter and my play
But a façade to cover the absolute stillness that I am

My words and my songs, my smiles and my mirth
Are but a ploy to entrap you in my limitless void

Both men and Gods were made in this void
O' Beloved if you dare, come - Dissolve.

One and the Same

The transparence of the morn'
Carries the fragrances of the birds chirping crystal clear!
What secrets they are transmitting
Is only between me and them
You would think it is of love, joy or just mundane needs
The sky and the birds are saying but
The one and the same
The plentiful and the barren are saying but
The one and the same
The flower and stone are saying but
The one and the same
All life, the moving and the unmoving are saying but
The one and the same

O'Shambho, how to make the fools know
You are but only me

The Dark One

When I first heard the sounds of
Darkness and silence meeting within me

The little mind argues for light
The virtue, the power, the beauty

Light a brief happening could hold me not
All encompassing darkness drew me in

Darkness the infinite eternity
Dwarfs the happened, the happening and yet to happen

Choosing the eternal
Darkness I became

The dark one that I am
The divine and the devil are but a small part

The divine I dispense with ease
If you meet the devil you better cease

Boundless

Home is the sailor, home from the seas,
Home is the farmer, home from the fields
Home is the hunter, home from the hills
In the twilight wonder I look up in the
Sky for a home, even the birds are homing.

Home, Home – Home for what?
Is it of brick and mud for security and shelter?
Or is it of love, companionship and comfort?
Homes of shelter and security or love and comfort
No homes for me.
Shambho my only Home
Homeless he is and Homeless am I
BOUNDLESS.

Himalaya

Even the rocks reach out to the heavens
No wonder beings seeking divine
Made you their abode

You of gushing waters and rushing airs
Towering presence of unsurpassable grace

The brave hands that crafted these paths
Into your ceaseless folds
A mighty effort but a miniscule

Many have traveled this labyrinth
That seemingly leads to your very womb

The womb that the courageous ones sought
To die and be born once again

These Dwijas – the twice born
Of immeasurable wisdom
Left imprints that even
The final deluge can erase not

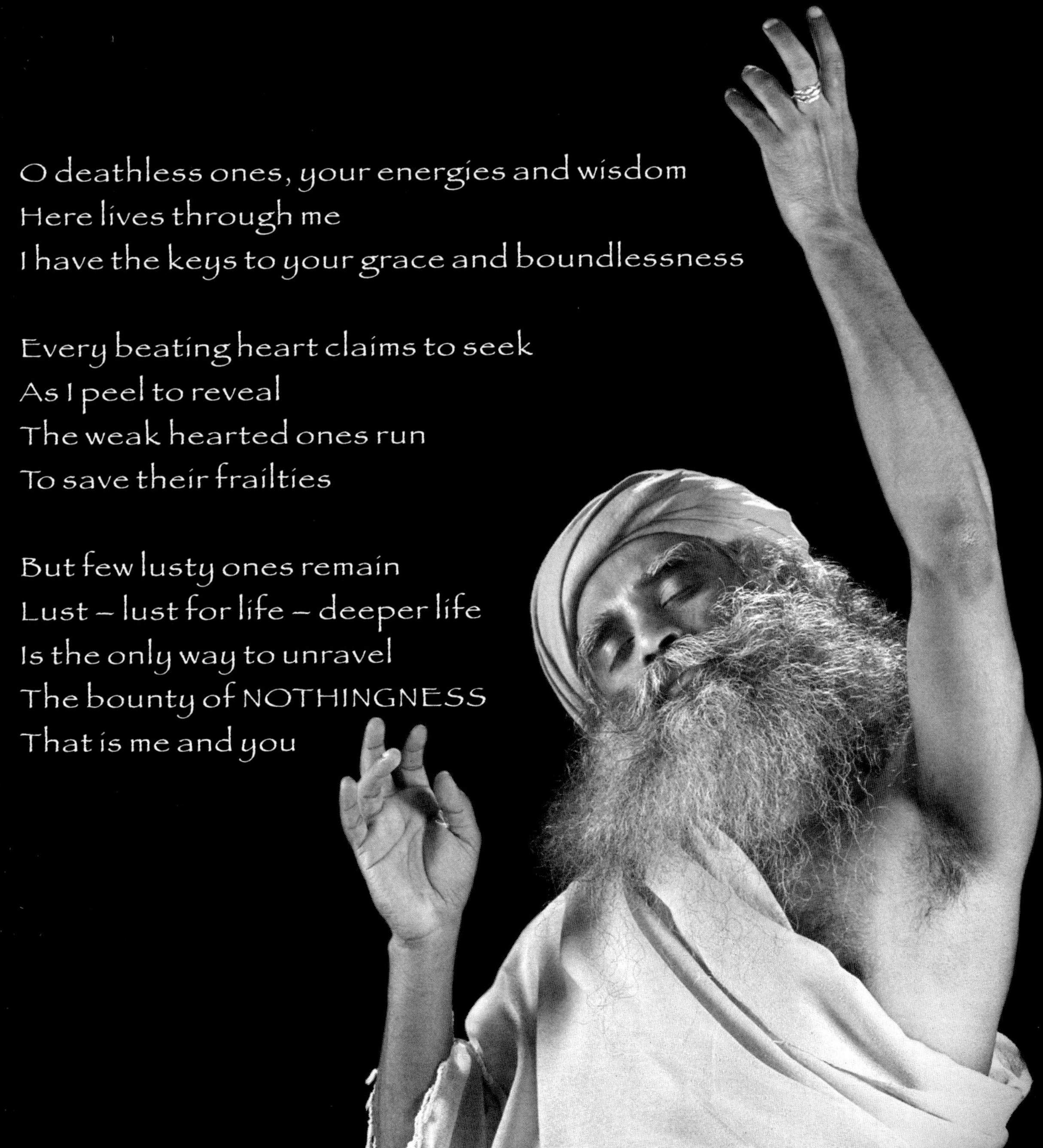

O deathless ones, your energies and wisdom
Here lives through me
I have the keys to your grace and boundlessness

Every beating heart claims to seek
As I peel to reveal
The weak hearted ones run
To save their frailties

But few lusty ones remain
Lust – lust for life – deeper life
Is the only way to unravel
The bounty of NOTHINGNESS
That is me and you

Island

You an island have become
An island large or small
But an island still
The stillness of the infinite will
Knocking on your door like a thrashing mill
But the robustness of your little pride
Could take you on an endless ride
You need to know it is just the hide
Peeling your own hide
Sure not an easy ride
Piece by piece if you tear
You will be unable to bear
Let this me get beneath your hide
In one piece it will fall by the side

Fall in step with my stride
For sure it will be an easy ride

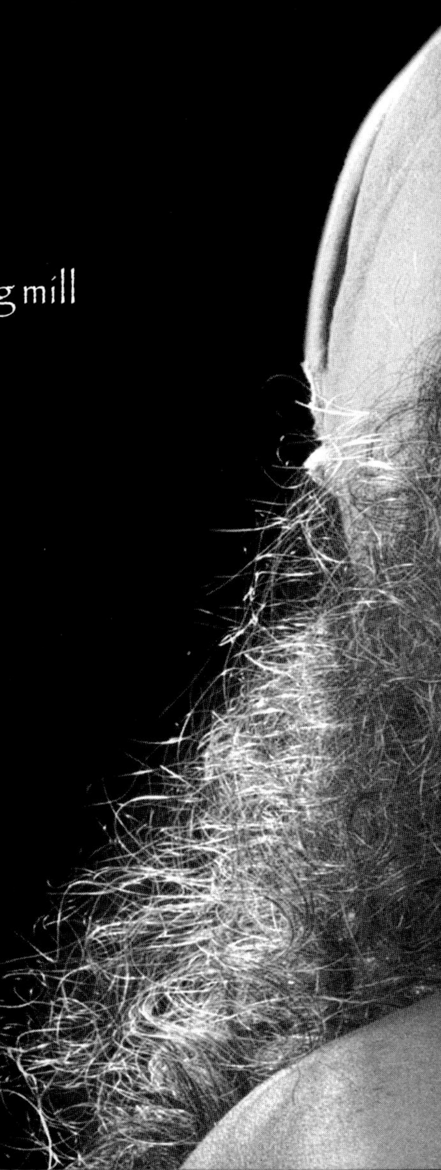

America

The brooding darkness of these woods
Fed upon the native blood
In the twisted tangle of the fallen wood
The spirit of the fallen Indian stood

O brothers your identity a mistake
Those who oceans crossed did make
The greed for gold and land
Laid waste the spirit of wisdom and grace

The children of those, who by murder did take
Are taintless of their forefathers mistake
But those who lived, fed upon the milk of courage and pride
Stand as spirits of defeat and shame

O the murdered and the murderous
Embrace me, let me set your spirits to rest

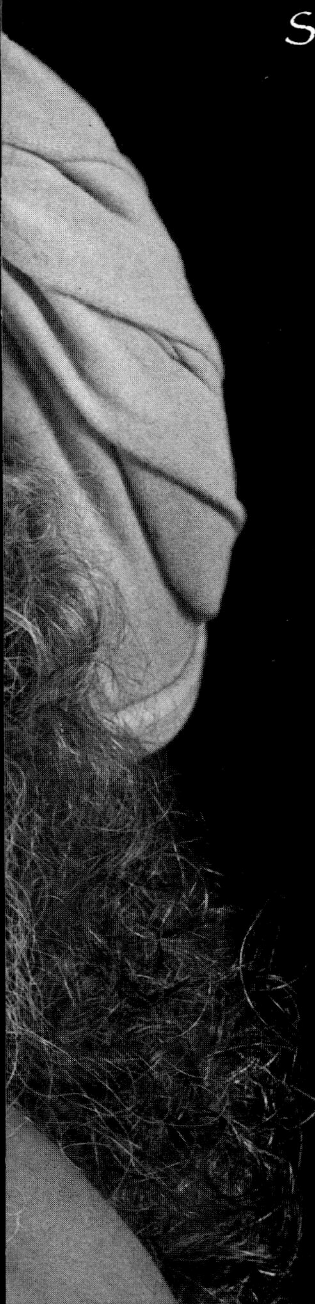

Shameless

Of virtue and shame
All arguments a game

The shamelessness of a slut
The lifeless copulation of glorified spouse
Of the shameless and the lifeless
Which a greater crime?

The strength of shoulder, of donkey in prime
Would make a well bred horse stand in shame
The left over plateful would make the beggar well
And leave the king in raging hell

The boundless being that I am
Know neither virtue nor shame

O virtuous of the world
Till you know the boundlessness of who I am
Shame, shame, it's all a crime

Empty

How shall I tell you
my predicament

Would thinking minds
ever know the brilliance in me
that would put the poor sun to shame
And it is not me

Would curious minds
ever know the ecstasy
that this grave visage masks
And it is not me

Would objective minds
ever know that these stern eyes could exude
love that could turn stones into beating hearts
And it is not me

Oh how shall I tell you
my predicament
I am empty but full

Inner Delight

The stark barrenness of the desert
Stood as mute reflection of my heart
The thirst of the parched tongue
Was puny to my heart's longing
The waterless dry death of the desert
Would be relief to my love's longing
This merciless longing
Not seeking any belonging

The toils of the endless day
The lonesomeness of the longer night
Amalgamated into brightness bright
Soaking me in an inner delight
The merciless longing and lack of belonging
Led me on into the wonderment of dissolving

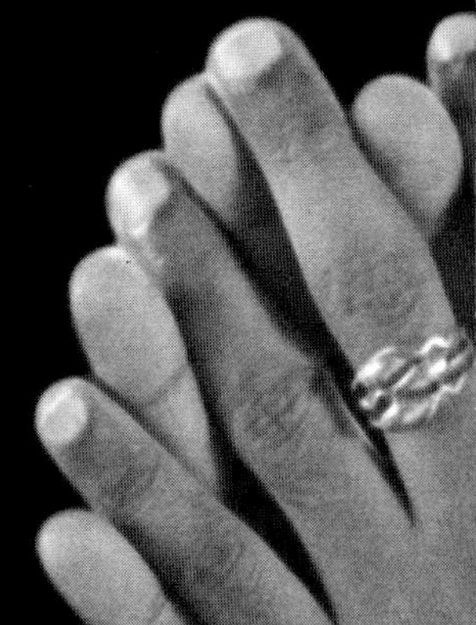

Life

The cool mountain breeze
Caresses me and the mountains
Cold, bare and blue
These ageless brooding rocks
Much life they have
Sustained, nourished and snuffed out

In your bosom you have borne
Men of gentle love and heartless treachery
Many a man has spilt blood
Upon you by accident or intent

The cool mountain breeze caresses me
Inviting to life and death

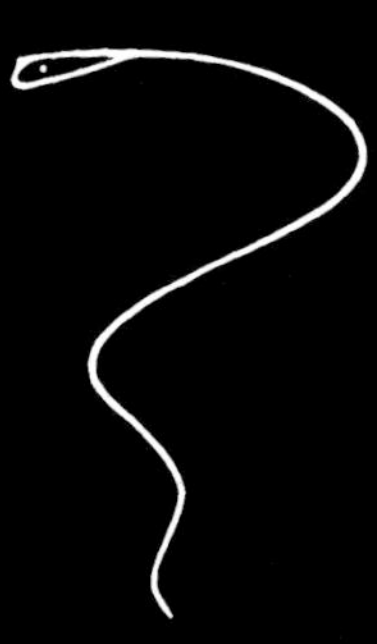

Benediction

Since time immemorial divine beings have graced the earth. Sadhguru Jaggi Vasudev can be described as just that. His work is an outpouring of his blissfulness that finds expression in the form of uninhibited compassion, love and a ceaseless offering to help all beings.

Belonging to no particular tradition, Sadhguru incorporates what is most valid for the modern seeker from the spiritual sciences. He offers yoga as the absolute potential to participate in the elusive mystery of existence.

The Master is a bridge to the Divine who offers humanity an opportunity and possibility to transcend the body and mind and experience the boundless divine bliss within.

He is available to all who are willing in ways beyond our logical understanding. His life is an invitation to individual transformation.

May you know the Divine.

Isha Foundation

Sadhguru developed Isha Yoga, The Soul of Yoga, as the vehicle to transmit a deep experience of the Self, which rooted three lifetimes ago and flourishes today as a spiritual science for hundreds of thousands of initiates around the world. Isha Foundation embraces the human effort to transcend physical reality in order to reach an inner reality, ultimate awareness, or enlightenment. This is the purpose of life itself.

Isha Foundation is an international public service organization which also administers the Dhyanalinga multi-religious temple and meditation shrine, an ashram and yogic hospital at the Isha Yoga Center, located on 50 acres at the foothills of the Velliangiri Mountains, 30kms from Coimbatore, India.

For worldwide programs and other Isha Foundation publications visit www.ishafoundation.org.

Isha Foundation,
15, Govindasamy Naidu Layout, Singanallur, Coimbatore – 641 005, India.
Telephone: 91-422-319655. Telefax: 91-422-319654.
Email: yogacentre@ishafoundation.org.

Isha Foundation, Inc.,
10, Belcaro Circle, Nashville, Tennessee - 37215, U.S.A.
Telephone: 615-665-3812, Telefax: 615-665-8326.
Email: info@ishafoundation.org.

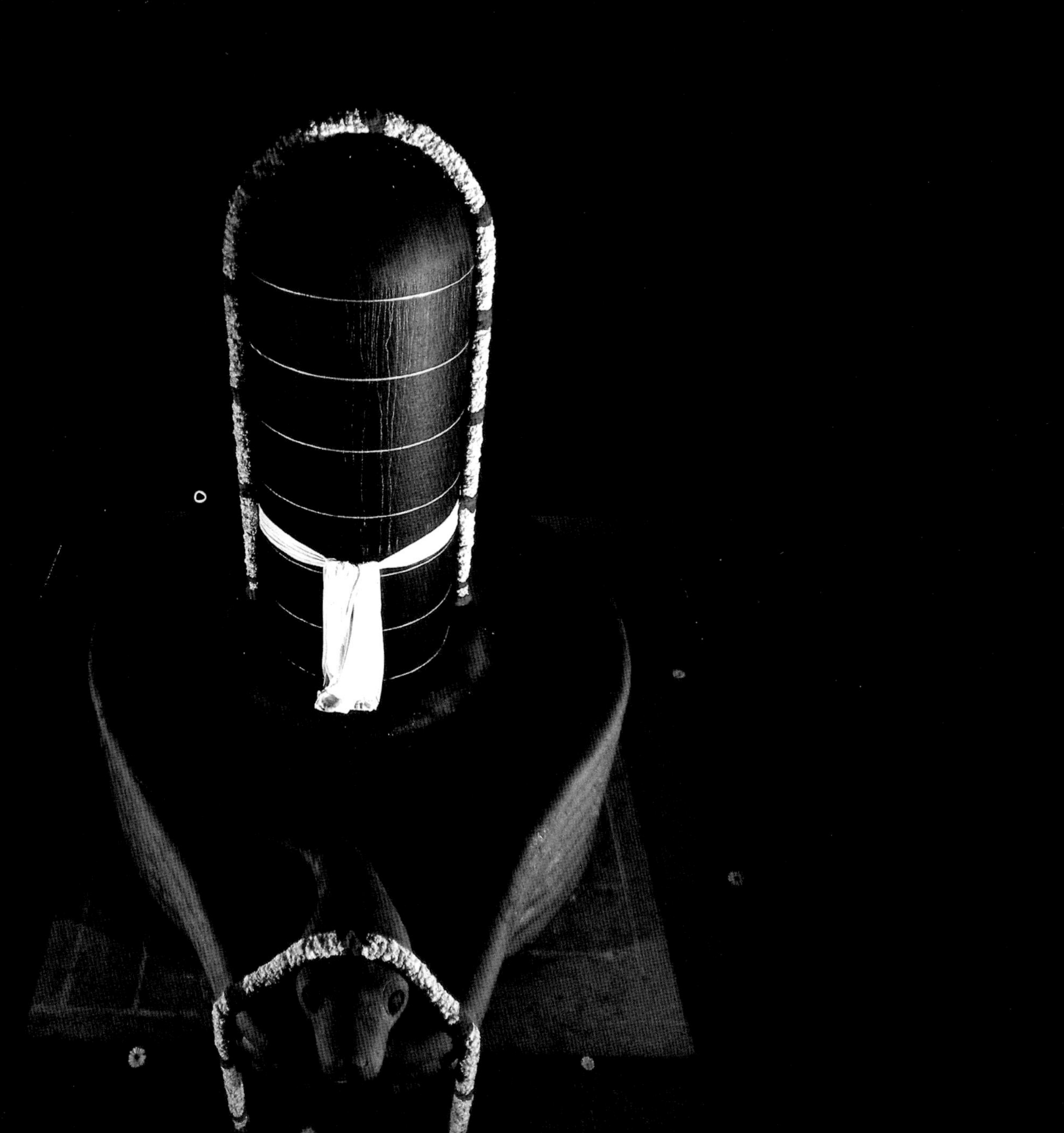

Dhyanalinga

On a certain afternoon, more than twenty years ago, sitting on a rock by himself in the Chamundi Hills in Mysore, South India, Sadhguru had a powerful spiritual experience that changed everything in his life. It brought back a flood of lifetimes of memories reminding him of his Guru's dream and his single-pointed purpose in life. Then on, every action he performed has been towards consecrating the Dhyanalinga, the dream of many Enlightened beings.

Dhyanalinga is the pinnacle of yogic sciences. It requires no faith, belief or worship. Just sitting silently for a few minutes in the sphere of the Dhyanalinga is enough to make even those unaware of meditation to experience deep states of meditativeness.

Anyone who comes within the sphere of the Dhyanalinga cannot escape the sowing of the spiritual seed of liberation. A doorway to Enlightenment and liberation, Dhyanalinga offers a sadhaka the opportunity to perform sadhana in utmost intimacy with a Guru, which is usually available only to a very few.

Situated at the foothills of the Velliangiri Mountains in South India, Dhyanalinga is enshrined in a brick dome - an engineering marvel, unique in its construction and material.

Isha

FOUNDATION

sacred space for self transformation